Scottie's
TEN
SNOWFLAKE
WISHES

INSTA@ ReadersMakeThinkers

SCOTTIE TODDLER BOOKS — PRESCHOOL BOOKS

An itty-bitty puppy was out on a walk,
Peeking inside row after row of decorated window shops.
At night when it was time for comfy sleep, he dreamt about what he saw
And tonight that included ten snowflakes from a soft snow fall.
Can you help the puppy count them all ?

xoxo The Author

WHERE IS THE PUPPY?

'Twas the night before Christmas and outside his puppy house,
a cuddly creature named Scottie was fascinated by ten
powdery snowflakes that moved as quiet as a mouse.

Trikes, trains, bears and blocks

filled the window of the **Toy Shop**.

And this is where Scottie saw

1 snowflake drop.

He wondered if it tasted like a

sugarplum, but when he went to lick it,

away it tumbled in a jolly bop.

Gallant soldiers in the **Nutcracker Shop** stood guard

overlooking the boulevard

as **2** snowflakes bounced softly, not hard,

off Scottie's ears before dashing

beyond a golden lamp

that glowed like a star.

Outside the **Drink Shop**, Scottie inhaled

the yummy scents of

hot cocoa, coffee and apple cider.

Then, 3 snowflakes tickled his nose before

they flew up higher & higher.

COCOA
MARSHMALLOWS
CANDY CANES
NOEL

4

Atop the **Coat Shop**, Scottie spied where

4 frosty snowflakes sat.

Scottie imagined wearing a new, snuggly hat.

One made him look like a reindeer,

another like a dapper chap.

But did any make him look like a cat?

In front of the **Art Shop**,

Scottie wagged his tail in a holiday prance.

His day was made brighter by the

many colorful paint palettes.

Even **5** glistening snowflakes gave

glad tidings as they chased pass.

The **Sweet Shop** had a shiny train

filled with yummy lollipops, chocolates

and candy canes.

Scottie daydreamed he'd munch on each

goodie again and again

while **6** snowflakes danced along the lane.

Over by the **Skate Shop**, Scottie's tiny

paws were laced in ice skates

as he twirled to reach for 7 snowflakes.

He couldn't wait

to catch one and celebrate.

At the **Puppy Stroller Shop**,

Scottie wondered if the buggies made a noisy

or a peaceful whirr.

Playing make-believe, he rode in one

while the wind brushed his fur

when he spotted 8 snowflakes

floating gently in the winter air.

Scottie jumped in front of the **Bake Shop** hoping

for a bite of the frosted cakes,

as well as a peek of the

Gingerbread Cookie trying to escape!

And rolling round the sidewalk were

9 sparkly snowflakes.

HOLLY JOLLY...
JOY
NOEL
PEACE

As his stroll along the avenue came to an end,
Scottie looked inside the **Bookshop** in awe of
big books, small books and the magical stories within
when drifting alongside him

were **10** cheery snowflakes on a night swim.

Scottie wanted to catch one. He slowly raised his top
lip to touch his nose at the brim,
but out slipped a yawn because
Scottie was ready to be tucked in.

Scottie tried to stay awake, but

after a sip from his puppy dish ~

he was snug in his warm bed remembering 10

snowflakes that twinkled white and bluish.

Scottie hummed softly as he made a sleepy wish:

To catch 10 snowflakes in his dreams is what he would accomplish.

Goodnight Scottie. Sleep cozy tonight

under silver bells, moonbeams and the twilight.

Until our next walk,

Merry Christmas to all
and
to all a goodnight !

Activity #1:

Trace the numbers with your finger.

Can you drag them on the mini snow blankets inside the box to their matching number?

Activity #2:

Cut out the 10 snowflakes on the next pages.

String together with yarn.

Now you have your very own snowflake garland.

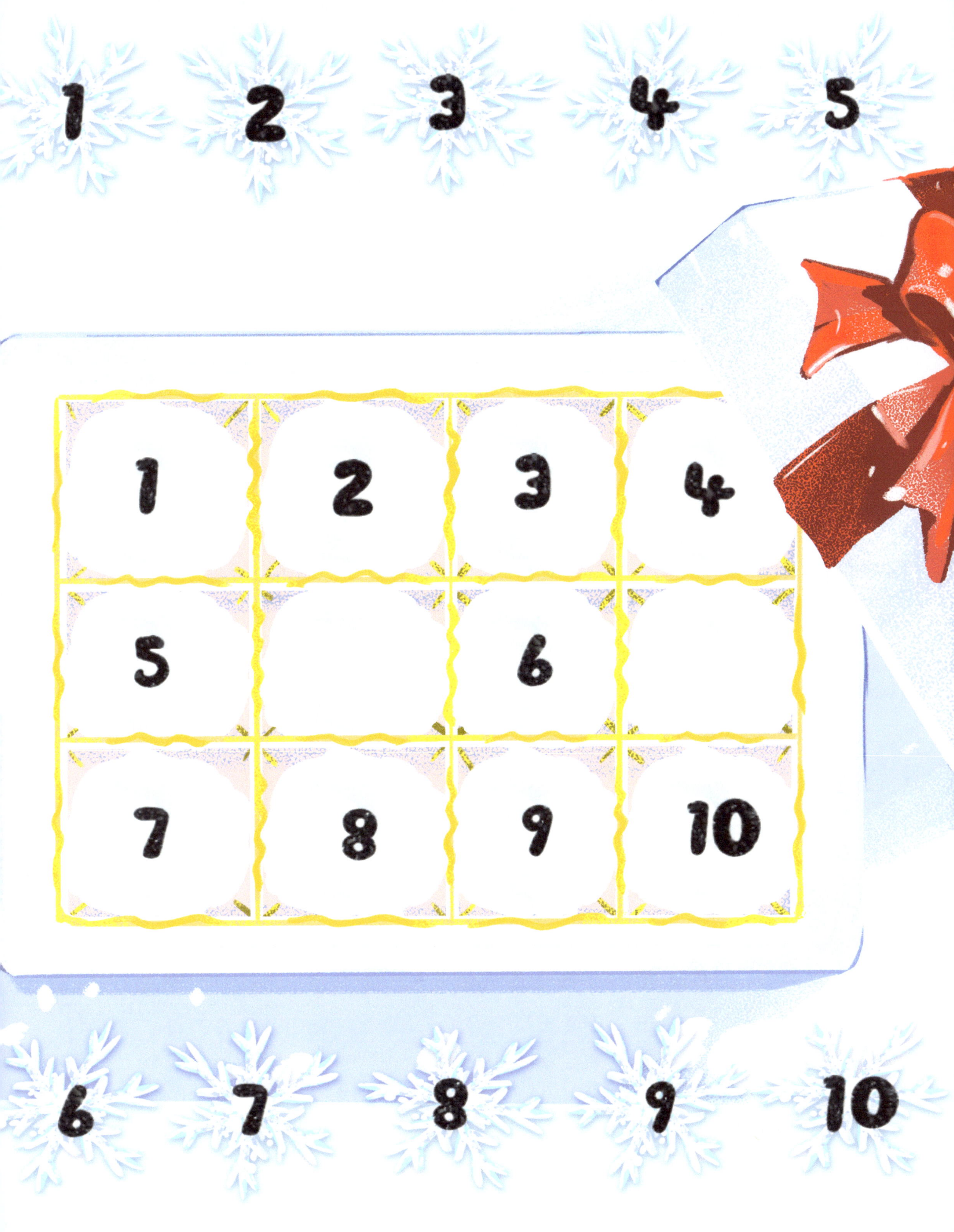

1 2 3 4 5
1 2 3 4
5 6
7 8 9 10
6 7 8 9 10

More from The Author

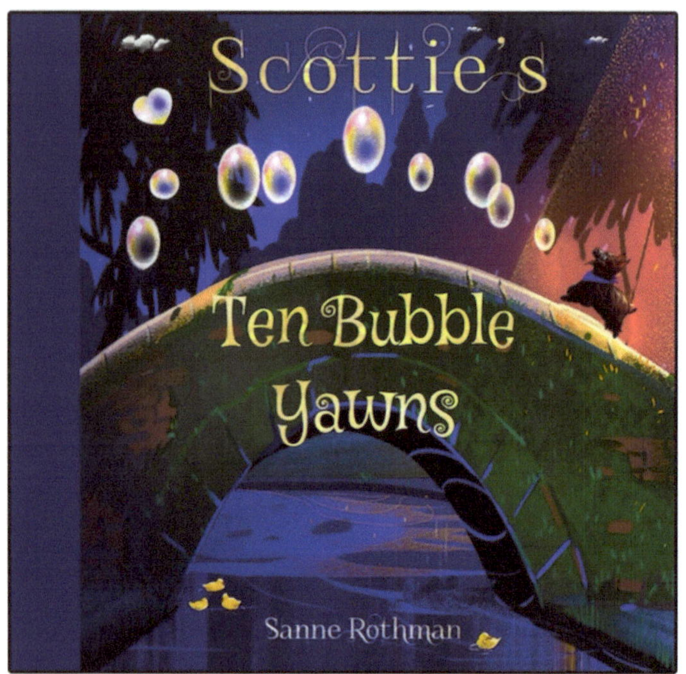

Scottie's
Ten Bubble
Yawns
Sanne Rothman

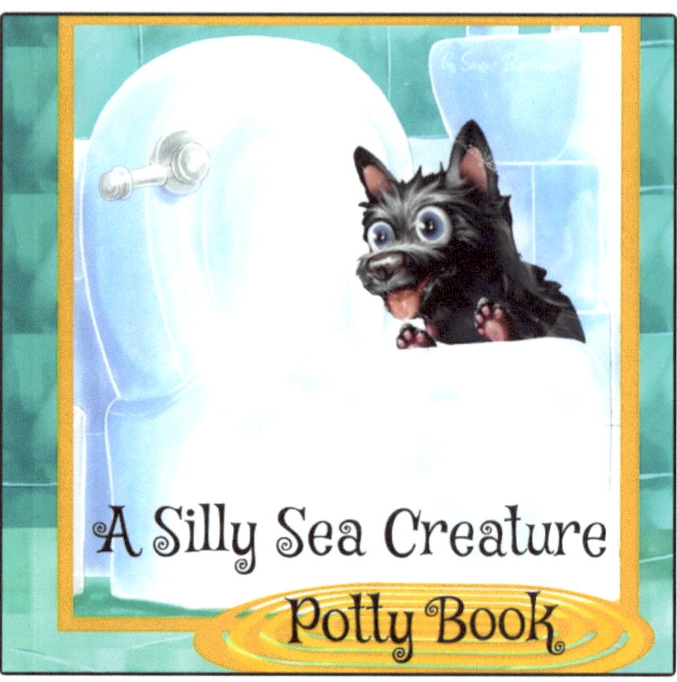

A Silly Sea Creature
Potty Book

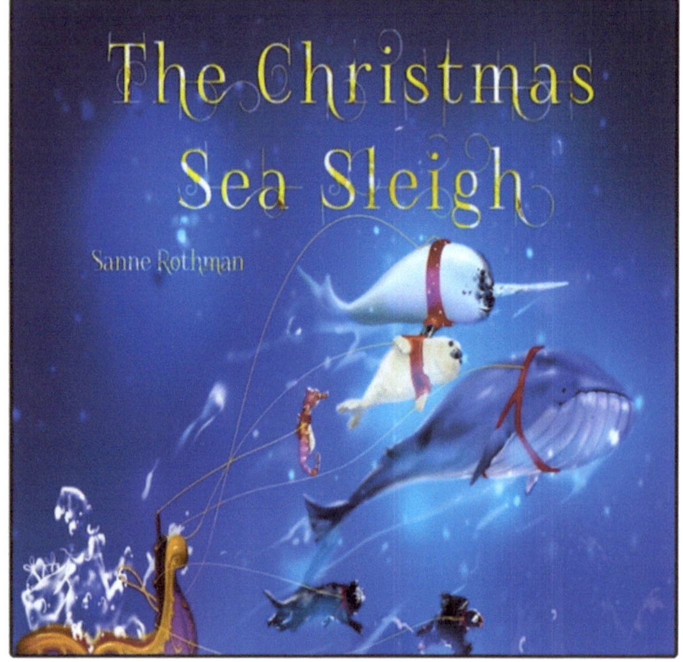

The Christmas
Sea Sleigh
Sanne Rothman

WHAT'S INSIDE THE CHRISTMAS TREE